BRITISH COACHING STOCK

BRITISH COACHING STOCK

John Dedman

AMBERLEY

Front cover: No. 33117 is leaving Eastleigh Depot with three Network SouthEast-liveried coaches on 7 June 1990. From the loco they are Mk 2A Corridor Brake First, Mk 2B Open Second and Mk 2B Corridor First.

Rear cover: The corridor side of RB No. M1733, which is in blue and grey livery with Commonwealth bogies when seen at Derby on 29 July 1978.

First published 2018

Amberley Publishing
The Hill, Stroud
Gloucestershire, GL5 4EP

www.amberley-books.com

Copyright © John Dedman, 2018

The right of John Dedman to be identified as the Author of this work has been asserted in accordance with the Copyright, Designs and Patents Act 1988.

ISBN 978 1 4456 7094 2 (print)
ISBN 978 1 4456 7095 9 (ebook)

British Library Cataloguing in Publication Data. A catalogue record for this book is available from the British Library.

Origination by Amberley Publishing.

Introduction

As a schoolboy trainspotter in the early 1960s, the various coach types always interested me. School summer holidays gave me a local Runabout ticket, which gave seven days of unlimited travel around South Hampshire, which I mostly used between Bournemouth, Southampton and Eastleigh. At the time there were many different coach types to travel in: BR Mk 1s, Southern Bulleids, Maunsells and occasionally some older non-corridor stock, which at the time were a complete mystery to me. The Southern system of coach sets also aroused our interest, giving us more numbers to collect. Unfortunately, none of my records from the period survived. I can remember noticing when the yellow band first appeared on first-class coaches and the red band on catering vehicles. A highlight from the period was a day at Bournemouth West, when we discovered that for about a two shilling supplement we could travel second-class in a Pullman on the Bournemouth Belle to Southampton. I'm not sure what the steward thought about two scruffy young teenagers, but he served us a couple of miniature packets of biscuits, which were all we could afford from the menu.

I first started to take photographs of coaches in the late 1970s, mainly as references for modelling purposes, and have been adding more images to my collection as the years have passed. My collection starts with BR Mk 1 coaches, which include many different types. As well as the regular day-to-day vehicles there are many photographs of various types of restaurant, kitchen, buffet and sleeping cars.

The Mk 1 coaches were followed by the XP64 prototypes in 1964, which were still in service in 1980, although by then they had been modified. These were followed by the first BR Mk 2 coaches, which are sometimes identified as Mk 2Z. These were the last coaches built with vacuum brakes, with air brakes being fitted to subsequent builds. From the late 1960s and through the 1970s, Mk 2A, B, C, D, E and F versions were introduced. Loco-hauled Mk 3 coaches are included in this collection, as is the Caledonian Sleeper, with its distinctive liveried Mk 3 sleeping cars and day coaches.

Pullman coaches fall into three main groups: the traditional cars, the Mk 1s, as used on the East Coast Main Line, and the Mk 2s, as used on the Manchester Pullman service. Examples of all three groups are still in service with various operators today.

I have been lucky enough to be in the right place to get some shots of the Royal Train and the opportunity to photograph some of the stock. For security reasons there is very little information on some of these coaches.

Non-passenger-carrying vehicles include Royal Mail Travelling Post Office sorting and stowage vans, Parcels vehicles, Inspection Saloons and some Network Rail test coaches.

Included are some photographs of older coaches still running on the main line today, which are usually seen in private charter and excursion trains. There are also photos showing how the trains are composed, which hopefully will be useful for railway modellers when making up their coach formations.

I would like to thank Steve Mosedale for the use of some of his photographs, as well as Mick Bryan and Mike Cole for their information.

Restaurant Second (RSO) No. E1066 is on the Poole to Newcastle service at New Milton on 24 December 1979. It is in blue and grey livery with the red cantrail stripe, as applied to all catering coaches of the period. Twelve of these restaurant cars were re-classified from diagram 73 Mk 1 Open Firsts in 1976 and all carried Eastern Region numbers. They were re-classified again in 1980 as Open Seconds.

RSO No. E1070 is another of the same batch. It is forty-two-seat restaurant car fitted with Commonwealth bogies and marshalled next to a RKB, which supplied the meals from its kitchen. Photographed at Southampton on 8 April 1980, it is on the Poole to Newcastle service.

Restaurant Unclassified Open No. E1036 is coded RUO and is seen in the carriage sidings at Newton Abbot on 21 May 1978. Built in 1961, this coach has seating for forty-eight diners and is fitted with Commonwealth bogies.

Green-liveried No. S1105 is preserved and in use on the Mid Hants Railway. Seen at Alresford on 7 August 2012, it is labelled 'Buffet' and is riding on B5 bogies. It was converted in 1965 from a Restaurant First into a griddle car to diagram 31 and was used in Scotland as No. SC1105. This was a small class of six coaches but there are two others preserved: No. 1100 on the Great Central Railway and No. 1104 on the Battlefield line, both of which are in BR maroon livery.

The Restaurant Kitchen Buffet (RKB) was not very common during British Rail days on the Southern Region but there was one regular working. This was the Poole to Newcastle Inter-Regional service, which was formed of Eastern Region stock. The train was composed of early Mk 2 coaches with RKB No. E1517 coupled to an RSO for dining. It is seen passing through New Milton on 2 February 1980. The Southern Region had an allocation of two RKBs, No. S1552 and No. S1553, which were allocated to Waterloo–Exeter services in the 1960s.

RKB No. M1525 is viewed from the kitchen side. It has B5 bogies and is in the standard blue and grey livery. These coaches had a kitchen and pantry with a buffet counter at the right-hand end but no seating as they were designed to be marshalled next to an open coach where meals could be served. It was in the formation of a northbound InterCity train on the West Coast Main Line (WCML) when seen at Bletchley on 15 August 1980.

Another view of a diagram 25 RKB. Viewed from the opposite end to the previous photo, this is No. M1554 as it passes Tring on 17 June 1982.

An unidentified RKB is in the formation of an Up service hauled by No. 47439 on the East Coast Main Line (ECML) when seen at Sandy on 14 September 1977. Seventy of these kitchen buffet coaches were built to diagram 25 and introduced in 1959. All were withdrawn by the end of the 1980s.

A view of the corridor side of an unidentified RKB in the formation of an Up WCML train, which was seen passing South Kenton on 7 April 1983. Although the rest of the coaches are Mk 3 and Mk 2, the catering coaches with kitchen facilities were still Mk 1.

The kitchen side of Restaurant Buffet (RB) No. M1635 at Bletchley on 15 August 1980. This coach seated twelve passengers and was converted in 1970 from a diagram 17 Restaurant First, which was built to diagram 28 in 1961 as No. M339. The difference in window and door arrangement can be seen in the following photo of RB No. M1644.

The kitchen side of diagram 24 RB No. M1644 at Wolverhampton on 24 August 1983. These coaches had a kitchen, pantry, buffet bar and seating for twenty-three passengers. The 'Buffet Restaurant' labelling is on the right end of the coach, whereas it was on the left end on the previous photo of No. M1635.

The kitchen side of RB No. S1766, seen at York in the formation of a day excursion from Brockenhurst on 17 March 1979. It is in the standard blue and grey livery with the label 'Buffet', and has Commonwealth bogies. There were only two of these loco-hauled RBs allocated to the Southern Region at this time, the other being No. S1765.

Buffet No. 1686 is a RB that has been refurbished and is now classified as RBR. It is in InterCity livery when seen at Stratford on 18 August 1994. It has Commonwealth bogies, small numbers on the lower right-hand bodyside and no 'Buffet' branding. It is on a Liverpool Street to Norwich service.

RBR No. 1683 is in Oxford Blue livery when seen at Carlisle on 16 July 2011. It is owned and operated by Riviera Trains and used mainly for excursion workings – in this case the 05.54 from Eastleigh to coincide with the Direct Rail Services Depot open day at Carlisle Kingmoor.

No. E1763 was built in 1961 as an RB but has been reclassified RBR. It is seen from the corridor side in blue and grey livery at Peterborough on 9 May 1981.

A train from the North East is heading south when seen at Bristol Temple Meads on 28 June 1980. Two catering vehicles are in use, with the buffet and kitchen in the RB, and tables for lunch in the RSO restaurant car. Both catering coaches have Commonwealth bogies.

RBR No. W1651 is in the early British Railways carmine and cream livery. It is owned and operated by Riviera Trains. It was built in 1960 and rides on Commonwealth bogies. It is at the Ocean Terminal in Southampton Eastern Docks on 28 December 2012 in the *Silent Witness* railtour, which also visited the Fawley and Hamworthy branches.

A pair of RBR cars seen in a Euston-bound train at South Kenton on 7 April 1983. The nearest one is ex-RU No. M1954 followed by ex-RB No. M1657, both of which are viewed from the corridor side.

The kitchen side of No. M1972 in a Down train at Tring on 17 June 1982. Built in 1961 as a diagram 23 RU with Commonwealth bogies, it has since been refurbished as a diagram 27 RBR with twenty-three seats. This can be identified as an ex-RU by noting the door between the kitchen windows, which did not exist on the RB.

No. E1937 is a 1957-built RU with a kitchen, pantry and seating for thirty-three diners. It is labelled 'Restaurant' and has Gresley bogies. It is seen in Derby on 29 July 1978.

Viewed from the kitchen side is RBR No. M1966 in blue and grey livery and with Commonwealth bogies. It started life as an RU but was refurbished and now contains a kitchen, pantry, buffet counter and seating for twenty-three passengers. It is seen in Derby on 29 July 1978.

RBR No. M1965 is seen at St Pancras on 29 July 1978. It is a similar coach to the previous photograph but is viewed from the corridor side.

Restaurant Miniature Buffet (RMB) No. M1869 was built in 1962 with Commonwealth bogies and is seen in standard blue and grey livery. It is in the formation of the 07.20 Liverpool Lime Street to Poole Inter-Regional as it passes Redbridge on 25 July 1984. These coaches are based on the Open Second, with five seating bays having been removed to accommodate the buffet counter and storage cupboard.

RMB No. 1879 is in the formation of the 12.38 Poole to Manchester as it approaches Southampton Central on 8 April 1988. It is in InterCity livery with the red band above the windows that denotes a catering vehicle and has Commonwealth bogies.

RMB No. 1842 is also in InterCity livery but is seen from the opposite side. The red band above the windows is only on the non-seating section of the coach. The train is a Norwich to Liverpool service and is seen at Ipswich on 16 July 1998.

RMB No. 1860 is in the maroon livery of West Coast Railways and is in use on main-line railtours. It is on the 'Dorset Coast Express' when it is seen, passing Eastleigh behind No. 70013 *Oliver Cromwell* on 4 September 2013.

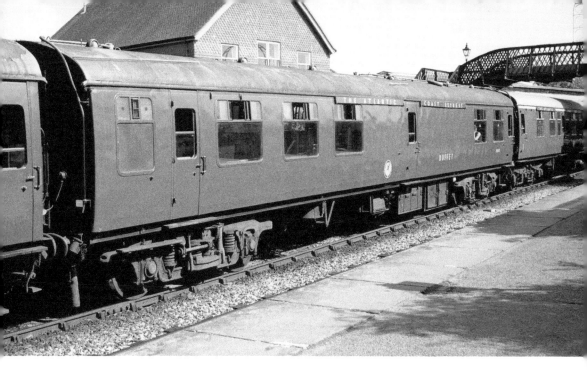

RMB No. S1818 is seen in BR Southern green livery at Sheffield Park on the Bluebell Railway on 15 August 1998.

SLF No. W2004 is a First-Class sleeping car in blue and grey livery. Running on B5 bogies it has eleven single-berth compartments and an attendant's compartment. The train is the Glasgow to Bristol overnight train and is seen on 19 February 1983 after arriving at its destination.

Another view of the Glasgow sleeper at Bristol on 28 June 1980, which shows the three different Mk 1 sleeping cars: a SLF first-class, No. W2003, a SLC composite, No. W2418, and a SLS second-class, No. W2550.

SLC No. W2420 is a composite sleeper car seen from the compartment side. It is in blue and grey livery and is again at Bristol on 19 February 1983. The compartments comprise of five singles for first-class and six doubles for second-class, plus an attendant's compartment.

In the same train is another composite sleeper, this time SLC No. W2423, which is seen from the corridor side at Bristol on 19 February 1983.

The compartment side of second-class sleeper car SLS No. W2546 at Bristol after arrival from Glasgow on 19 February 1983.

SLS No. M2430 is at Brockenhurst on 8 June 1980. It is one of the two second-class sleeper cars on the Stirling to Brockenhurst Motorail service, which has just arrived behind No. 33015. It has B5 bogies and is seen from the compartment side, which has one window per compartment.

Another view of the same train shows the corridor side of an unidentified second-class sleeper car after arrival at Brockenhurst behind No. 33050 on 22 May 1977.

No. W3150 was built as an Open First, coded FO, and has since been downgraded to an Open Second, coded SO. It has forty-two seats with two on one side of the gangway and one on the other, which makes it an attractive ride for anyone travelling second-class. It is in blue and grey livery, has a toilet compartment at either end, and has Commonwealth bogies. It is seen at Reading on 24 March 1984.

Carmine and cream-liveried Mk 1 First Open No. M3097, seen here in an empty stock working to Crewe, is at Eastleigh on 4 December 2012. It is owned and operated by Riviera Trains and used for railtours.

Mk I Open First S3069 is in the formation of a railtour at Southampton Eastern Docks on 28 December 2012. It will have visited this location many times in the past as part of the Ocean Liner boat train from Waterloo. It is in 1950s carmine and cream livery, which it probably carried when it was first built in 1955. Current livery additions are the British Railways coach crest, the yellow band denoting first-class and the orange cantrail lining. It is owned by Riviera Trains, has B4 bogies and carries a Royal Scot board.

Mk I Tourist Open Second (TSO) No. 4880 was built in 1960 and has sixty-four seats and B4 bogies. It is in Regional Railways livery and is seen on the rear of the morning Birmingham International to Holyhead as it leaves Stafford on 7 April 1998.

Regional Railways-liveried Mk 1 TSO No. 4917 is at Crewe on 13 August 1996. It is on the rear of a Regional Railways service from Holyhead.

TSO No. 5029 is in service with Regional Railways but in late 1950s Western Region livery, with the British Railways roundel crest on the bodyside. It has Commonwealth bogies and is on the rear of a Birmingham to Bangor service on 13 August 1996.

Second Open No. M4643 has BR Mk 1 bogies and is in BR maroon livery with gold and black lining. It is at Llangollen on 16 June 2015.

BSO No. M9208 is a Brake Second Open with five seating bays in the saloon, giving a total of forty seats. It is seen here at Bristol Temple Meads on 28 June 1980 as the last passenger coach of a passing Motorail train.

An unidentified BSO is heading north on the West Coast Main Line and is seen at Tring behind No. 81019 on 26 August 1982. It is in standard blue and grey livery and has BR1 bogies.

Corridor First FK No. W13346 is at Peterborough on 9 May 1981. It has Commonwealth bogies, is in blue and grey livery and is seen from the corridor side. It has three external doors on this side and only two on the compartment side.

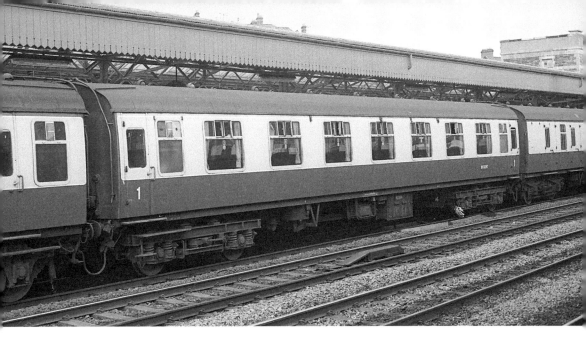

FK No. W13297 is viewed from the compartment side. It is riding on B4 bogies and has seven compartments, each seating six passengers with a toilet at each end of the coach. It is at Newport on 7 February 1981 in the 10.15 Portsmouth Harbour to Cardiff service hauled by No. 31401.

The Motorail from Stirling has arrived at its destination at Brockenhurst on 8 June 1980. After unloading its passengers in the station, it is reversing into the vehicle unloading dock. The train is made up of two SLS, one FK, one BFK and the car flats. This was half of the train that left Stirling the previous evening; the other half went to Dover after the train was divided in West London.

A closer view of the four passenger coaches with the Brake First nearest. BFK No. W14025 has Commonwealth bogies and is showing its compartment side. It is marked 'Motorail Not to Exceed 90 mph' on the end of the coach. Beyond are the corridor side of the FK and two second-class SLS sleeping cars. The empty coaching stock will head to Bournemouth for servicing before returning in the evening for its run to Scotland.

The corridor side of BFK No. W17025 is shown at Southampton on 8 April 1988. It has four passenger compartments, a toilet compartment, guard's facilities and luggage space. With Commonwealth bogies, it is in the formation of a Cardiff to Portsmouth Harbour working.

The Corridor Composite coach had four compartments seating twenty-four first-class passengers and three compartments seating twenty-four second-class passengers with a toilet compartment at either end. Some of these coaches were built with armrests in the second-class compartments, which meant they only seated eighteen second-class passengers. CK No. M15989 is seen at Southampton on 8 April 1980 in an Inter-Regional working.

Corridor Composite CK No. W7215 is seen from the corridor side at Dawlish Warren when bringing up the rear of a Down local stopping train. It is in standard blue and grey livery and has Commonwealth bogies.

Blue and grey-liveried Corridor Composite No. W7124 is seen from the compartment side. The four first-class compartments are indicated by the yellow stripe above the windows. The centre compartment of the three second-class compartments has the stretcher window, which has a wider frame. The train is the 07.20 Liverpool Lime Street to Poole Inter-Regional, which is seen passing Redbridge on 25 July 1984.

The Corridor Brake Composite (BCK) coach had two first- and three second-class compartments, two toilets, luggage space and a guard's compartment. BCK No. W21034 is seen from the compartment side on a Portsmouth Harbour to Cardiff service near Southampton on 2 April 1983.

Corridor Brake Composite BCK No. E21219 is viewed from the corridor side at Bristol on 28 June 1980. These coaches could seat twelve first-class passengers or, depending on whether armrests were fitted, eighteen or twenty-four second-class passengers.

The compartment side is shown on BCK No. W21185 at Bristol on 28 June 1980. The two first-class compartments have curtains whereas the three second-class compartments have pull-down blinds. These coaches were quite easy to identify with their smaller than normal brake end and the yellow lining for the first-class section being in the centre of the coach.

Corridor Second SK No. 18775 looks abandoned at Reading on 28 November 1987. It is in Network SouthEast livery with one of its corridor windows missing. It is fitted with Commonwealth bogies and contains eight second-class compartments, which could seat sixty-four passengers. There are toilet cubicles at both ends of the coach.

No. M25743 is preserved at Toddington on the Gloucester and Warwickshire Railway. This Corridor Second is in British Railways lined maroon livery. Previously, it was in service with Network SouthEast in blue, red and white livery. It is seen here on 27 June 2006.

BSK No. 35452 is a Corridor Brake Second in Regional Railways livery with Commonwealth bogies. These coaches had four passenger compartments, a guard's compartment and a large luggage area. (Steve Mosedale)

No. 33029 with the 16.10 Portsmouth Harbour to Cardiff Central at Millbrook on 15 April 1983. These trains were normally four or five coaches; on this occasion, it has four Mk 1s – BSK, TSO, CK and TSO.

No. 31403 is heading north at Winwick with four Mk 1 coaches on 13 June 1990. The first is a BSK Corridor Brake Second in blue and grey livery followed by three Network SouthEast-liveried second-class coaches. All are on Commonwealth bogies.

A diagram 702 kitchen car from the number series M80029–39 is included in an excursion set returning north from Bournemouth. Built in 1962 and riding on B5 bogies, it is seen at New Milton on 16 June 1979.

Kitchen car No. M80042 was converted from RBR No. 1646 and is now coded RK. The buffet and seating area has been removed and replaced with more kitchen area. In the formation of the 5Z21 15.32 Southampton Western Docks to Eastleigh, it is seen at its destination on 30 June 2012. It was the empty stock of the 1Z20 06.08 Glasgow Central to Southampton Western Docks boat train, which was hauled by No. 67026.

The XP64 coaches were introduced in 1964 and were the first to carry the blue and grey livery. There was only eight of these prototype coaches built, consisting of three different types. Open Second No. W4728 is at Beaulieu Road in the New Forest on the rear of the Cardiff to Weymouth train on 23 June 1979.

SK No. W25508 is one of a pair of XP64 Corridor Second coaches. It has eight compartments with the side corridor changing sides at the centre of the coach. Unusually, this coach lacks a door at the left-hand end; rather, it has one at the right-hand end and one in the centre of the coach, which is the same on the other side. It is at Bristol on 28 June 1980 in the 08.15 Cardiff to Portsmouth Harbour.

XP64 Corridor Second SK No. W25508 is seen at Bristol on 28 June 1980 in the 12.15 Portsmouth Harbour to Bristol. These coaches were originally built with wider folding doors, but they were modified at Wolverton in 1970 and 1971 to have standard outward-opening doors.

SK No. W25509 is the other XP64 Corridor Second coach, which is shown here at Bristol on 28 June 1980.

FK No. W13407 is one of the three XP64 Corridor First coaches. It has seven compartments with a side corridor, which switches sides near the centre of the coach. Like the second-class coaches, the original wide folding doors have been replaced with standard-width doors. It is in the formation of the summer Saturday Cardiff to Bournemouth and is seen at Sway on 5 August 1978.

Open Second No. 5236 is a forty-eight-seat Mk 2Z coach with B4 bogies. These coaches, with their forty-eight seats instead of the sixty-four seats found in a TSO, were suitable for use as restaurant cars when marshalled next to a kitchen car. It is in green livery at Brockenhurst on 16 August 2006 when in service with West Coast Trains on a railtour.

Mk 2A TSO No. 5347 is in the attractive Trans-Pennine livery. It has B4 bogies, seating for sixty-four passengers and was built in 1968. It is seen here at Thornaby Depot on 1 October 1988.

Regional Railways-liveried Mk 2A TSO No. 5419 is at Stafford on 7 April 1998. These coaches were used in services between Birmingham, Crewe and North Wales in four- and five-coach rakes with a mix of Mk 1 and Mk 2 coaches. (Steve Mosedale)

TSO No. W5341 is in carmine and cream livery, which is unusual for a MK 2 coach. It is owned and run by Riviera Trains. It is passing through Eastleigh on Friday, 8 May 2009 en route from Eastleigh Depot to Southall for a railtour the following day.

No. 47471 *Norman Tunna G.C.* is crossing the Kent Viaduct at Arnside with the 2J92 Saturdays-only 9.00 Barrow-in-Furness to Manchester Victoria on 31 October 1992. The five-coach Mk 2 formation is made up of three TSOs with a BSO at either end – all of which are looking very attractive in Regional Railways livery.

No. 37418 *East Lancashire Railway* is departing Crewe with the 10.24 to Bangor on 8 June 1995. The five-coach formation consists of two Mk 2A TSOs, one Mk 2A BSK and two Mk 1 TSOs. The whole train, wearing Regional Railways livery, is spoilt by the BSK, which is in Network SouthEast livery with the red stripe removed.

No. 31426 is seen arriving at Lancaster with the 2J68 13.18 Barrow to Manchester Victoria on 12 July 1990. The coaches are a Mk 2A TSO and a Mk 1 TSO, which are in Network SouthEast livery, and a Mk 1 BSK and a Mk 1 TSO, which are in blue and grey livery.

BR blue and grey-liveried No. W5439 is a Mk 2B TSO. It can seat sixty-two passengers, has a toilet compartment at either end and can be identified from the Mk 2A as it has wrap-around end doors, but no centre door. It is the first coach in the 13.35 Exeter to Waterloo behind No. 50050 *Fearless* and is seen at Southampton on 9 March 1985. This was diverted due to weekend engineering work.

No. S9392 is a Mk 2Z BSO Open Brake Standard. This coach has the same bodyshell as the Mk 2 BFK but has thirty-two seats. It is owned and operated by the West Coast Railway Company and is in their standard red livery. Recorded at Eastleigh on 26 November 2009, it is part of a Poole to Bristol steam-hauled railtour.

Mk 2A Corridor First No. 13440 was built in 1968. It has B4 bogies and seven compartments to seat a total of forty-two passengers. It is owned and operated by the West Coast Railway Company and is seen at Brockenhurst in a railtour on 16 August 2006. By this date it was the only one of its type left in main-line service as the railtour companies preferred to use open coaches.

BFK No. 17096 is in Network SouthEast livery at Southampton on 8 April 1988 as part of the formation of the 11.05 Exeter St Davids to Waterloo, which has been diverted due to engineering work on its normal route. This Mk 2A coach has B4 bogies and four compartments to seat twenty-four first-class passengers, as well as containing a guard's compartment and luggage space.

No. 17056 is a Mk 2A Corridor Brake First that was built in 1967. It has B4 bogies and is in EWS Maroon livery with gold/black/gold waist lining. It is owned and operated by Riviera Trains. Seen at Eastleigh on 30 June 2012, it is in the 5Z40 17.05 Eastleigh Depot to Chichester empty coaching stock train behind Royal-liveried No. 67005. This coach has since been repainted into carmine and cream livery and is owned by Locomotive Services.

No. 35513 is a Mk 2A Corridor Brake Standard that has been re-numbered from BFK No. 17063. It is in Regional Railways livery, has B4 bogies and carries twenty-four passengers. These coaches were used in services between Birmingham, Crewe and North Wales. The set on this occasion were Nos 5309, 5322, 35513 and 5420. It is seen at Stafford on 7 April 1998. (Steve Mosedale)

The 1M51 08.15 Nottingham to Blackpool North is passing Toton Depot hauled by No. 47407 on 8 July 1989. The set of eight Mk 2 coaches are a Mk 2A BSO, a Mk 2C TSOT, a Mk 2C SK, a Mk 2A SK, two Mk 2C SKs, a Mk 2A TSO and a Mk 2A BSO. The TSOT is a TSO with a micro-buffet added in place of one of the seating bays and with a steward's area in place of one of the toilets. The Mk 2A SK and the three Mk 2C SKa were all downgraded and re-classified from Corridor Firsts.

In 1988 and 1989 some Mk 2F Open Firsts were converted to Buffet Open First, being coded RFB. They were allocated to InterCity Cross-Country to replace Mk 1 buffet cars. No. 1203 is in InterCity livery and is on the tail end of a Cross-Country train at Stafford in 1997. (Steve Mosedale)

Mk 2F RFB No. 1208 is in Virgin Trains livery when seen at Reading in 1999 on a Cross-Country train heading for Poole. These coaches have B4 bogies, seating for twenty-six passengers and one toilet compartment. No. 1208 was converted from FO No. 3393. (Steve Mosedale)

An unidentified ScotRail-liveried Mk 2D TSO is a long way from home when seen on the South Coast at Eastleigh on 14 September 1985 as part of a northbound Inter-Regional from Poole to Glasgow.

No. 5789 is an InterCity-liveried Mk 2E TSO seen at Reading in 1998. It has B4 bogies, sixty-four seats and two toilet compartments, which are diagonally opposite each other so they are always at the right-hand end when looking at the coach side. (Steve Mosedale)

Viewed from the opposite side is Mk 2E TSO No. 5847, which is in Virgin Trains livery. Both this and the previous photo were allocated to Virgin CrossCountry. (Steve Mosedale)

No. 6134 is a Mk 2F TSO that is in InterCity livery with B4 bogies. It is seen at Southampton in a Cross-Country working in 1998. (Steve Mosedale)

Mk 2F TSO No. 6177 is still in Virgin Trains livery when seen at Eastleigh on 4 December 2012. It is in a Riviera Trains railtour set when seen leaving the depot and heading for Crewe.

Anglia Railways-liveried No. 3295 is an air-conditioned Mk 2F Open First, which is seen at Eastleigh on 4 December 2012. It has forty-two seats and two toilet compartments, which are both on the side of the coach in view.

The same coach, No. 3295, is shown from the opposite side at Carlisle on 16 July 2011. It is owned by Riviera Trains and on this day is in the formation of a railtour from Eastleigh for a visit to the DRS Depot open day at Carlisle Kingmoor. These coaches are very popular with railtour operators and are often used for at-seat catering.

Mk 2F FO No. 3348 was built in 1973 and has since been refurbished. It is in Riviera Trains blue and cream livery with gold lining and is named *Gainsborough*. It is in the same railtour as the previous photo when seen at Carlisle on 16 July 2011.

No. M9505 is an air-conditioned Mk 2F Open Brake Second in blue and grey livery with B4 bogies. These coaches were built in 1972 with seating for thirty-two passengers, one toilet, a guard's compartment and a large luggage area. It is seen at Wolverhampton on 24 August 1983.

Built two years later was BSO Mk 2F No. 9522, which is seen in InterCity livery. It is at Reading in 1998 in a Cross-Country service. (Steve Mosedale)

Another BSO Mk 2F coach of the same batch is No. 9525, which is seen in Virgin Trains livery at Didcot in a CrossCountry service in 1998. (Steve Mosedale)

Mk 2F BSO No. 9537 is in Cruise Saver Express advertising livery for use on the boat train from Glasgow and Edinburgh to Southampton Docks to connect with cruise ships. It has had all its seats removed to make more room for luggage. It is seen at Carlisle on 16 November 2011.

A view from the other end of Cruise Saver Express BSO No. 9537 at Carlisle on 16 November 2011. The ship is the Cunard liner *Queen Elizabeth*.

Mk 3A RFM No. 10254 is a Restaurant Buffet First that is seen in InterCity livery with BT10 bogies at Stafford on 7 April 1998.

No. 11006 is an air-conditioned Mk 3A Open First in InterCity livery built in 1975. It was converted in 1985 to Open Composite for use in Scotland and re-numbered 11906. It was later converted back to Open First in 1990 with forty-eight seats and two toilet compartments. It is seen at Stafford on 7 April 1998. (Steve Mosedale)

Mk 3A TSO No. 12063 is in InterCity livery when seen at Stafford on 7 April 1998. (Steve Mosedale)

No. 87015 *Howard of Effingham* is seen heading north from Crewe at Coppenhall with a set of InterCity-liveried Mk 3 coaches on 11 July 1997. There are five TSOs, a buffet, two FOs and a driving van trailer.

Mk 3A sleeper car No. M10535 is viewed from the corridor side at Allerton Depot on 22 July 1984. It is classified as SLEP – Sleeper Either class with Pantry. It has an attendant's compartment and twelve sleeping compartments, which have a fixed lower berth and hinged upper berth, meaning they can be used for single occupancy for first-class passengers.

No. 10551 is a Mk 3A SLEP. It is in First Group ScotRail Caledonian livery. It is seen from the compartment side at Crewe on 10 July 2010 in a late-running 1M16 Inverness to Euston overnight train with sleeper cars from Aberdeen and Fort William having been added at Edinburgh.

No. 10507 is a similar SLEP, also seen at Crewe on 10 July 2010, but is viewed from the corridor side.

No. 10688 is a SLE Mk 3A sleeper car with thirteen compartments with similar berth arrangements to the SLEP. The train is viewed from the corridor side at Crewe on 10 July 2010.

Another SLE is No. 10703, which is viewed from the compartment side at Crewe on 10 July 2010 in the Inverness to Euston overnight train. This heavy overnight service is composed of sixteen coaches and on this day the formation comprises Nos 10551, 10722, 10597, 10703, 10548, 10714, 1220, 9803, 10507, 10688, 10502, 10513, 10527, 10718, 6706, 9804, which are hauled by No. 90026.

BUO No. 9803 is an Unclassified Open Brake coach. It has been converted from a Mk 2E TSO for use on the sleeper trains. Eleven of these conversions were made in 1999, providing the coaches with thirty-one reclining seats, guard's accommodation, a luggage area and two toilets. It is seen from the corridor side at Crewe on 10 October 2010.

BUO No. 9806 is seen from the opposite side at Fort William on 24 April 2009 after arrival from Edinburgh.

No. 1220 is a Buffet First converted from a Mk 2F First Open in 1989. It is seen at Crewe on 10 July 2010.

RLO No. 6706 is an air-conditioned Sleeper Reception Car also seen at Crewe on 10 July 2010. This is also a conversion from a Mk 2F Open First. It has been fitted with a pantry, staff facilities and new seating for thirty passengers.

Pullman car *Bertha* is part of the Bluebell Railway's Golden Arrow dining car train, which is seen at Sheffield Park on 15 August 1998. *Bertha* was one of a group of composite kitchen cars with first- and second-class seating. One of these cars was included in the Southern's 6-PUL six-car electric multiple units. *Bertha* is now undergoing restoration at Carnforth and will eventually go to the Swanage Railway.

Pullman car *Ione* is an all-steel 'K' type first-class kitchen car from 1928. It was used on the Great Western until 1931, when it transferred to the Southern, where it remained until 1939. After the Second World War it was used in Pullman services on the East Coast Main Line from Kings Cross until withdrawal in 1968. It was refurbished in the early 1980s for the Venice-Simplon Orient Express (VSOE). On 4 August 2009 it is in the formation of the 08.45 from London Victoria as it crosses Canute Road into Southampton Eastern Docks.

Cygnus is a Pullman Parlour First and was built in 1951 for the Golden Arrow. It has Gresley bogies and is part of the VSOE on a luncheon trip from Bournemouth, where it is seen passing Millbrook on 21 October 2011.

Pullman Kitchen First *Gwen* was built in 1932 and was originally one of the Brighton Belle coaches. It has been converted as hauled stock and is included in the VSOE at Millbrook on 21 October 2011.

Pullman car No. 14 was one of two observation cars used on the Devon Belle between London Waterloo and Ilfracombe from 1948 to 1954. This coach went to America with the Flying Scotsman in 1969. It finally returned to the UK in 2007 for the Swanage Railway, where it was refurbished and put back into service. It is shown here at Corfe Castle on the rear of a service heading for Swanage on 1 April 2017.

Opal is a Mk 1 Parlour First, which was first put into service in 1961 on the East Coast Main Line Pullman trains working out of Kings Cross. It was withdrawn from service in 1978 after use on the Hull Pullman, where it ran in the reversed blue/grey livery. It is now preserved on the North Yorkshire Moors Railway, where it has been restored to its original Pullman livery. It is shown here at Grosmount on 12 June 2002.

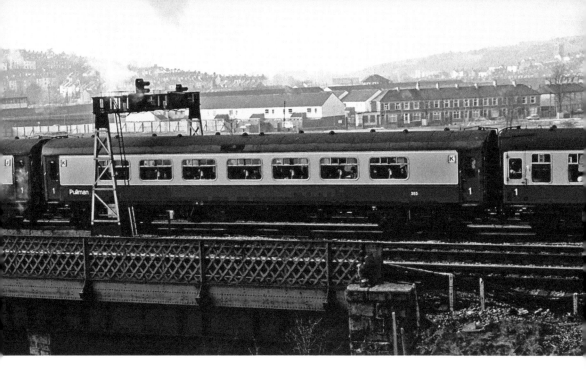

Mk 1 Pullman car No. 353 is in BR blue grey livery in the formation of a steam-hauled special at Newport on 19 February 1983. It has been re-classified from Parlour Second to Open First.

Pullman Parlour Second No. 350 is in the same train at Newport on 19 February 1983 but it is in traditional Pullman livery.

Car No. 350 is in use with West Coast Railways in their maroon livery and is numbered 99350. It is at Eastleigh on 4 September 2013 in the Dorset Coast Express, which is hauled by No. 70013.

By 2017, No. 99350 had been repainted back into its original Pullman livery and named *Tanzanite*. It is still in service with West Coast Railways and is at Appleby on 20 May in the formation of the 1Z87 14.40 Carlisle to Euston, being hauled by No. 46115 *Scots Guardsman* on the same steam-hauled railtour.

Mk 1 Pullman *Topaz* is at Appleby on 20 May 2017. It is in the same steam-hauled railtour as *Tanzanite* in the previous photo. This coach was originally Parlour Second No. 348.

An unidentified Class 86 is heading north near Linslade with the Down evening Manchester Pullman on 15 August 1980. Behind the loco is a brake van (BG) followed by seven Mk 2 Pullman coaches: a brake, a kitchen, two parlours, a kitchen, a parlour and the final brake. The reverse blue and grey livery was standard for the Mk 2 Pullman coaches.

No. 86220 *Goliath* with the 07.33 Manchester Piccadilly to Euston Manchester Pullman at Tring on 26 August 1982. The stock is composed of six Mk 2 Pullmans with a Mk 1 blue and grey BG on the rear, which is replacing a Pullman brake.

Parlour First coaches seen on the Down morning Manchester Pullman at Bletchley on 15 August 1980.

Pullman Kitchen First (PFK) No. M500 is seen on the Down morning Manchester Pullman at Tring on 17 June 1982. This shows the kitchen side of the coach; there was seating for eighteen passengers at the far end.

Mk 2 Pullman *Windermere* is in service with West Coast Railways. It was originally Kitchen First No. M506 and has been painted into traditional Pullman livery. It is departing from Crewe on a railtour on 10 July 2010.

The rear of the Down morning Manchester Pullman as it leaves the Watford Junction stop on 7 April 1983.

The rear of the Down morning Manchester Pullman as it leaves the Watford Junction stop on 30 January 1985. The Mk 2 Pullmans are now in the latest InterCity livery with the Brake First on the rear of the set. These coaches were all given names when repainted into this livery.

No. 86233 *Laurence Olivier* is seen at Linslade on 30 September 1986 with an Up Pullman service from Manchester. The train is composed of Mk 3 Pullmans. The catering is supplied from the second coach, which is a MK 1 RKB, and the sixth coach, which is a blue and grey-liveried Mk 3 catering coach. Bringing up the rear is a Mk 1 BG that is also in blue and grey livery.

No. 73142 *Broadlands* is seen with the Royal Train at Southampton on 4 August 1983. The No. 96 headcode shows it is heading for the Western Docks. As it is only a five-coach train it is probably transporting members of the Royal Family from London to a ship. The five coaches are Nos 2906, 2902, 2900, 2907 and 2905.

No. 2906 is a royal staff vehicle. It was converted in 1977 from Mk 2B BFK No. 14112, which was built in 1969 with B4 bogies. It contains a diesel generator, guard's compartment, luggage area and staff sleeping accommodation. It is seen here on 4 August 1983.

No. 2902 is a royal dining saloon, which was built in 1956 and is seen at Southampton on 4 August 1983. Its original number was No. M499 and it was re-numbered in 1977 to No. 2902. The photograph was taken from the kitchen end with the dining area at the other end of the coach.

No. 2900 is a royal saloon, which was built in 1955. It contains a lounge, four bedrooms and a bathroom. It is normally used by members of the Royal Household.

Restaurant First (RF) No. 2907 is included in the Royal Train, which is seen heading for Southampton Western Docks on 4 August 1983. This coach was built as No. M325 in 1961 in BR maroon livery and spent a few years as part of the Royal Train until it was repainted in Royal Claret livery in 1977. It was re-numbered in 1982 from No. M325. It originally had Commonwealth bogies, which were later replaced with B5 bogies.

The Royal Train is passing Southampton Maritime Freightliner Terminal behind No. 67006 *Royal Sovereign* when seen on 27 October 2016 on its journey from Dorchester to London. The coaches are Nos 10546, 2920, 2915, 2917, 2916, 2923, 2922, 2904, 2903 and 2921, with No. 67005 *Queen's Messenger* on the rear. The first coach, No. 10546, is a Mk 3a sleeping car with a pantry in EWS maroon livery. The remaining coaches are all in the Royal Train livery of claret with red and black lining.

No. 2920 is one of the brake coaches for the Royal Train. It was converted from Mk 2B BFK Corridor Brake First No. 17109 in 1986. B5 bogies have been fitted and the coach contains a diesel generator, staff sleeping accommodation and the guard's compartment.

No. 2915 is a Mk 3A sleeping car for the use of the Royal Household. It is seen at Southampton on 27 October 2016.

Royal Kitchen Household Dining Car No. 2917 was converted in 1990 from High Speed Train Mk 3 Restaurant Kitchen TRUK No. 40514.

No. 2916 is HRH the Prince of Wales's dining car, which is seen on 27 October 2016. It was originally Mk 3 No. 40512, a TRUK in a High Speed Train. It was converted in 1988 for use in the Royal Train.

Royal Saloon No. 2923 is a Mk 3B. It was built in 1987 with BT10 bogies and is seen at Southampton on 27 October 2016.

No. 2922 is HRH the Prince of Wales's sleeping car, which is also a Mk 3B built in 1987 with BT10 bogies. It is seen at Southampton on 27 October 2016.

No. 2904 is HRH the Duke of Edinburgh's saloon. It was converted in 1977 from No. 12001, a Mk 3 Open Second, and has both living and sleeping accommodations. It is seen at Southampton on 27 October 2016.

No. 2903 is HM the Queen's saloon. This coach started life in 1972 as Mk 3 Open First No. 11001 and was converted in 1977 to its present condition. It has BT10 bogies and is fitted with double doors at one end. It is seen at Southampton on 27 October 2016.

The second brake coach of the Royal Train is No. 2921, which was converted from Mk 2B BFK No. 17107 in 1990. It is seen at Southampton on 27 October 2016.

NSA No. 80386 is a diagram 726 sorting van, with the Rail Express Systems logo having been added to the lower right bodyside. It is seen stabled at Carlisle in 2000. (Steve Mosedale)

NSA No. 80395 is another of the same type of coach as above but is seen stabled with the sliding doors open. The sorting desks were on the opposite side, where there was only a personnel door. (Steve Mosedale)

NTA No. 80436 is a diagram 727 stowage van, which is seen at Carlisle in 2000. These vans had three sets of sliding doors on each side. (Steve Mosedale)

NSX No. 80333 is a diagram 729 sorting van, which was originally fitted with nets and arms for collecting and dropping mail bags at the lineside. This was discontinued in 1971 and the equipment recess has been plated over. It is seen at Cardiff on 1 March 1995.

NSA No. 80337 is another diagram 729 sorting van, which was built with the provision for nets and arms but they were never fitted. This van is seen at Carlisle in 2000. (Steve Mosedale)

Two Travelling Post Office (TPO) vans are at the front of the 1M14 22.00 Stranraer to Euston Sleeper. The train loco is No. 86242 and the two vans were added at Carlisle. The second van is No. M80331, a diagram 729 sorting van. The photograph was taken at Tring on 17 June 1982.

NSX diagram 731 sorting van No. 80345 is stabled at Cardiff Central during the day on 26 May 1994. This livery with the large yellow lettering replaced the corporate image blue and grey in 1986.

In 1990 the yellow lettering was changed to white with new labelling, as seen on NSA No. 80345. This is another diagram 731 van, which is seen at Carlisle. (Steve Mosedale)

The other side of a diagram 731 sorting van, which just has a single personnel door. It is No. 80345, seen at Crewe on 14 August 1996.

NTA No. 80422 is a diagram 732 stowage van with three sliding doors on both sides, which is stabled at Carlisle in 2000. (Steve Mosedale)

No. 86212 *Preston Guild 1328–1992* is at Winwick on 26 October 1992 with a southbound mail train. Behind the loco is a blue and grey BG, a red Royal Mail BG, a diagram 729 TPO sorting van and two Royal Mail stowage vans.

NLA No. 94025 was converted from a General Utility Van (GUV) to a newspaper van with the addition of a toilet, gangways and B5 bogies. After the end of newspaper traffic it was used in Royal Mail trains and was re-painted into red livery with yellow lining. It is seen passing through Newport in a mail train on 26 May 1994.

NOA No. 95734 was originally a General Utility Van (GUV) but has been modified and re-classified as a High-Security GUV. It has been fitted with Commonwealth bogies, the centre doors have been sealed up and two roller-shutter doors have been fitted to each side. It is finished in plain Royal Mail red livery with no lining. (Steve Mosedale)

Another High-Security GUV is NKA No. 94164 in Rail Express Systems livery. This former GUV has been fitted with three roller-shutter doors on each side and the original end doors have been removed. It is seen here at Warrington on 10 August 1998.

No. 47757 *Restitution* in Rail Express Systems (RES) livery has five vans in tow and is southbound when seen at Coppenhall on 19 August 1997. There are three GUVs with a Super BG (brake van) on either end, all of which are fitted with roller-shutter doors and are in matching RES livery.

BG NEA No. 92959 is in Royal Mail red livery with yellow stripes. It has been fitted with B4 bogies and is on the tail end of a mail train at Cardiff on 1 March 1995.

BG No. 92229 has the TOPS code NEA and is in plain red livery. It was built in 1956 with BR1 bogies, which have been replaced with B4 bogies for 100 mph running. Here it is seen at Crewe in use in a mail train on 14 August 1996.

NCX No. 95229 is a BG that was modified to carry newspapers. It is in Rail Express Systems livery and has Commonwealth bogies. No longer in use for carrying newspapers, it is in the formation of a mail train at Cardiff on 1 March 1995.

NBA No. 94411 is a Super BG in Rail Express Systems livery with B4 bogies, which is seen at Carlisle in 2000. (Steve Mosedale)

Super BG No. 94538 is in DB Schenker maroon livery and is fitted with B4 bogies. It is being used to provide luggage space on the Glasgow to Southampton Western Docks DB Schenker boat train. It is at Eastleigh on the empty stock working from the docks on 30 June 2012.

BG NEX No. 92369 has been fitted with Commonwealth bogies for 100 mph running. Its blue and grey paintwork is very faded when photographed in a bay platform at Doncaster in 1999. (Steve Mosedale)

No. 31142 is heading south at Clay Cross Junction on 4 July 1985 with two ex-works coaches: an air-conditioned Mk 2 Open First and a Mk 1 BG. The BG is NEA No. 92195, which has been fitted with B4 bogies for 100 mph running.

NFV No. S245 is a 28-ton bogie guard's van built by the Southern Railway in 1939 at Eastleigh. The Southern classified it as van B. It has wooden panels and sits on SR bogies. It is seen at Bristol Temple Meads on 28 June 1980 as part of a parcels train. The last of these vans were withdrawn in 1986, although a small number were then taken into departmental service.

Southern Railway-designed, wooden-panelled, 25-ton scenery/general utility van No. S4606 was built in 1949. The van is coded NIV; it is in plain blue livery and is on the rear of a Class 31-hauled Bristol to Weymouth service at Bathampton Junction on 31 March 1978. The steam leaking from under the van shows this was a steam-heated train and that the loco boiler is still working well.

Inspection Saloon No. KDW150266 was an early 1960s conversion from an H33 restaurant coach, which was carried out at Swindon for the S&T Department at Reading. It is seen leaving Westbury behind No. 31404 on 11 June 1987.

Inspection Saloon No. TDB975025 is on display at the Andover Rail Event on 22 March 1986. This coach was converted in 1969 from buffet car No. S60755 from a Class 203 Hastings six-car unit, which was built at Eastleigh in 1958. It was used on 29 July 1981 to transport HRH Prince Charles and Diana, Princess of Wales from Waterloo to Romsey at the start of their honeymoon.

No. 975025 is now in green livery after a few years in Network SouthEast livery. It has also been named *Caroline*. It is being propelled north at Cossington on the Midland Main Line by No. 37422 on 22 June 2016. The narrow body of the ex-Hastings line coach can be seen in this view.

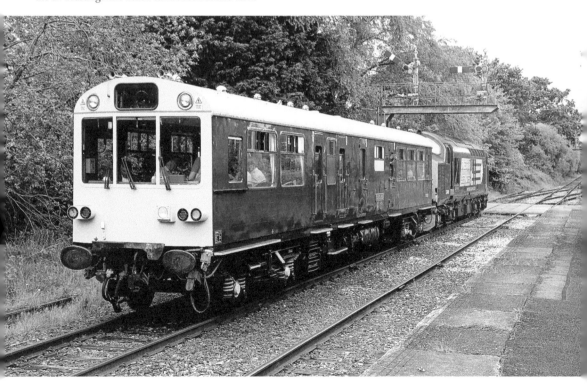

The other side of No. 975025 *Caroline* is shown at Marchwood on its return from an inspection of the Fawley branch on 16 May 2017 behind DRS No. 37409 *Lord Hinton*.

Inspection Saloon No. 999503 is in Regional Railways livery when seen at Warrington on 18 August 1993. This vehicle is one of a batch of five built in the late 1950s to an LMS design. Another of the batch, No. 999504, is preserved at the Ecclesbourne Valley Railway.

Inspection Saloon No. DB999508 was built at Swindon in the early 1960s and was rebuilt in 1987 as a Track Inspection Coach (TIC), which included the recessed side sections, headlights and cameras. It is in Serco red and grey livery with B4 bogies when seen at Ipswich on 16 July 1998.

Track Recording Coach No. DB999508 is at Southampton on 15 February 2010. It was re-painted into Network Rail livery in 2005. The driving positions are no longer used as it is marshalled in a top-and-tail formation with a loco at either end of the train.

No. 31233 is at Eastleigh with the 1Q43 test train on its return from Weymouth on 26 July 2012. It is composed of Nos 999508, 977969, 72639 and 72616 with 31106 on the rear. Nos 72639 and 72616 are brake force runners that were converted from ex-Gatwick Express Mk 2F TSOs, No. 6070 and No. 6007 respectively.

Network Rail yellow-liveried No. 977969 is a staff coach for use on Network Rail test trains and is seen at Eastleigh on 26 July 2012. It started life as Mk 2B Corridor Brake First No. 14112, which was later converted for use in the Royal Train, numbered as No. 2906. It was subsequently converted into No. 977969.

No. 73107 is leading the 1Q40 09.20 Selhurst to Eastleigh Network Rail test train, which is turning into Totton Yard, where it will reverse on 5 July 2010. The coaches are Nos 977868, 6261, 977983, 999550 and 977969 with 31465 on the rear.

Radio Survey Coach No. 977868 was converted from Mk 2E TSO No. 5846. It is included in the test train in the previous photograph at Totton on 5 July 2010.

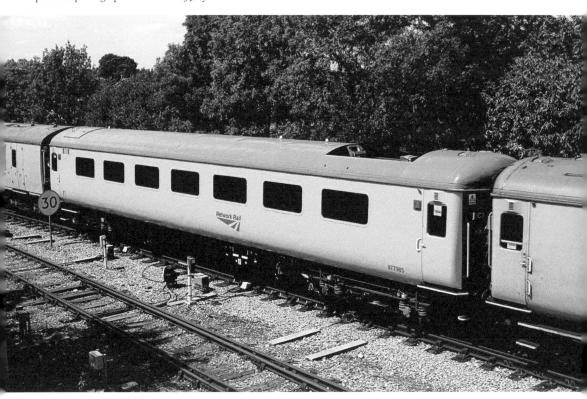

In the same test train is Track Recording Train Electrification Measurement Coach No. 977983, which was converted from Mk 2F FO No. 72503. This had previously been converted from No. 3407.

No. 999550 is a purpose-built Track Recording Coach; it was the final Mk 2 coach when built in 1977. Now in Network Rail yellow livery, it had previously been in BR blue/grey Research livery and Serco red/grey livery. It is also seen at Totton on 5 July 2010.

QVA No. ADB977107 is a part of the Eastleigh re-railing train. It was converted from BCK No. 21202 into a living and brake van. As well as the crane, there are two other coaches in the train, which are the tool van and the jacking van. The train is on display at Eastleigh Works open day on 12 October 1986.

Bibliography

Books

Harris, M., *British Rail Mark 2 Coaches*

Marsden, C. J., *Rolling Stock Recognition: Coaching Stock V. 1* (Littlehampton Book Services Ltd, 1987)

Parkin, K., `*British Railways Mark 1 Coaches*

Pritchard, R., *British Railways Locomotives and Coaching Stock*, Platform 5 Publishing Ltd (various editions)

RCTS, *British Rail Coaching Stock 1978, 1980, 1982*

Magazine

Modern Railways magazine, July 1964

Websites

Vintage Carriage Trust at www.vintagecarriagestrust.org

VSOE at www.kentrail.org.uk/index.htm